HEBREWS

REFORMED EXPOSITORY BIBLE STUDIES

A Companion Series to the Reformed Expository Commentaries

Series Editors

Daniel M. Doriani
Iain M. Duguid
Richard D. Phillips
Philip Graham Ryken

1 Samuel: A King after God's Own Heart
Esther & Ruth: The Lord Delivers and Redeems
Ecclesiastes: Enjoyment East of Eden
Song of Songs: Friendship on Fire
Daniel: Faith Enduring through Adversity
Matthew: Making Disciples for the Nations (two volumes)
Luke: Knowing for Sure (two volumes)
John: The Word Incarnate (two volumes)
Galatians: The Gospel of Free Grace
Ephesians: The Glory of Christ in the Life of the Church
Philippians: To Live Is Christ
1 Timothy: Defend the Faith
Hebrews: Standing Firm in Christ
James: Portrait of a Living Faith
1 Peter: Grace-Driven Discipleship in a Difficult Age

HEBREWS

STANDING FIRM IN CHRIST

A 13-LESSON STUDY

REFORMED EXPOSITORY
BIBLE STUDY

JON NIELSON
and **RICHARD D. PHILLIPS**

P.O. BOX 817 • PHILLIPSBURG • NEW JERSEY 08865-0817

All boxed quotations are taken from Richard D. Phillips's *Hebrews* in the Reformed Expository Commentary series. Page numbers in quotations refer to that source.

ISBN: 978-1-62995-755-5 (pbk)
ISBN: 978-1-62995-756-2 (ePub)
ISBN: 978-1-62995-757-9 (Mobi)

Printed in the United States of America

CONTENTS

SERIES INTRODUCTION

Studying the Bible will change your life. This is the consistent witness of Scripture and the experience of people all over the world, in every period of church history.

King David said, "The law of the LORD is perfect, reviving the soul; the testimony of the LORD is sure, making wise the simple; the precepts of the LORD are right, rejoicing the heart; the commandment of the LORD is pure, enlightening the eyes" (Ps. 19:7–8). So anyone who wants to be wiser and happier, and who wants to feel more alive, with a clearer perception of spiritual reality, should study the Scriptures.

Whether we study the Bible alone or with other Christians, it will change us from the inside out. The Reformed Expository Bible Studies provide tools for biblical transformation. Written as a companion to the Reformed Expository Commentary, this series of short books for personal or group study is designed to help people study the Bible for themselves, understand its message, and then apply its truths to daily life.

Each Bible study is introduced by a pastor-scholar who has written a full-length expository commentary on the same book of the Bible. The individual chapters start with the summary of a Bible passage, explaining **The Big Picture** of this portion of God's Word. Then the questions in **Getting Started** introduce one or two of the passage's main themes in ways that connect to life experience. These questions may be especially helpful for group leaders in generating lively conversation.

Understanding the Bible's message starts with seeing what is actually there, which is where **Observing the Text** comes in. Then the Bible study provides a longer and more in-depth set of questions entitled **Understanding the Text**. These questions carefully guide students through the entire passage, verse by verse or section by section.

It is important not to read a Bible passage in isolation, but to see it in the wider context of Scripture. So each Bible study includes two **Bible Connections** questions that invite readers to investigate passages from other places in Scripture—passages that add important background, offer valuable contrasts or comparisons, and especially connect the main passage to the person and work of Jesus Christ.

The next section is one of the most distinctive features of the Reformed Expository Bible Studies. The authors believe that the Bible teaches important doctrines of the Christian faith, and that reading biblical literature is enhanced when we know something about its underlying theology. The questions in **Theology Connections** identify some of these doctrines by bringing the Bible passage into conversation with creeds and confessions from the Reformed tradition, as well as with learned theologians of the church.

Our aim in all of this is to help ordinary Christians apply biblical truth to daily life. **Applying the Text** uses open-ended questions to get people thinking about sins that need to be confessed, attitudes that need to change, and areas of new obedience that need to come alive by the power and influence of the Holy Spirit. Finally, each study ends with a **Prayer Prompt** that invites Bible students to respond to what they are learning with petitions for God's help and words of praise and gratitude.

You will notice boxed quotations throughout the Bible study. These quotations come from one of the volumes in the Reformed Expository Commentary. Although the Bible study can stand alone and includes everything you need for a life-changing encounter with a book of the Bible, it is also intended to serve as a companion to a full commentary on the same biblical book. Reading the full commentary is especially useful for teachers who want to help their students answer the questions in the Bible study at a deeper level, as well as for students who wish to further enrich their own biblical understanding.

The people who worked together to produce this series of Bible studies have prayed that they will engage you more intimately with Scripture, producing the kind of spiritual transformation that only the Bible can bring.

Philip Graham Ryken
Coeditor of the Reformed Expository Commentary series

INTRODUCING HEBREWS

There is a scene from Jesus's ministry that wonderfully depicts the **main theme** of the book of Hebrews. In Matthew 17, we are told that Jesus took his three closest disciples onto the mount, where they saw him being transfigured in glory and speaking with Moses and Elijah. Peter, one of the disciples, proposed that a tabernacle be built for the veneration of these three spiritual giants. Just then, however, the shekinah glory cloud enveloped them in brightness and the voice of God sounded: "This is my beloved Son, with whom I am well pleased; listen to him" (Matt. 17:5). When the disciples rose from their terror, they saw neither Moses nor Elijah, but Jesus alone. So it is in the book of Hebrews, which highlights the supremacy of Christ in his person and work and presents faith in him as being necessary for salvation.

Hebrews contains the most concentrated Christology—doctrine of Christ—in all the New Testament. Yet it was written not as a theological text. It is, instead, a sermon in letter form—its author describes Hebrews as "my word of exhortation" (Heb. 13:22). The situation of his **audience** is made clear by the contents of the message. They were Jewish Christians who were experiencing persecution from the community in which they lived because of their faith in Jesus as the Son of God and promised Messiah. To be Christian meant repudiating their Jewish heritage, they were being told—making them traitors to their people. For them to join the church thus risked their expulsion from the synagogue, along with all the dire social implications this involved. Although they had not yet suffered violent persecution (see Heb. 12:4), they were experiencing social, economic, and relational exclusion from the society in which they had been raised. It is clear that powerful arguments were being leveled against their faith in Christ—all with the aim of persuading these Christians to deny

Jesus and regain social acceptance. In answer to this threat, the writer of Hebrews reminds his readers that there is no salvation apart from faith in Christ. The aim of Hebrews is therefore to encourage and exhort harassed Christians to remain faithful to their Lord, regardless of the cost.

It is not difficult to imagine the kinds of arguments that were being employed to dissuade these followers of Christ from their new faith. Playing on the fact that these believers, who were living in the mid-first century A.D., had not personally seen or heard Jesus, the Jews argued that he was only a man—the son of a poor carpenter from a backwater village. Jesus was an enthusiast in times of unrest, and his failure as Messiah was proved by his death on a cross—a humiliating execution that marked him as the worst sort of criminal. The real problem came when his deluded followers made outlandish claims that Jesus had risen from the grave and when they actually worshiped him as God. These were potent arguments—especially when they were enforced with such painful social affliction.

Against challenges like these, the writer of Hebrews begins by noting the continuity between Christianity and the Old Testament faith of his readers' fathers: "Long ago, at many times and in many ways, God spoke to our fathers by the prophets, but in these last days he has spoken to us by his Son" (Heb. 1:1–2). Christianity is not a repudiation of Old Testament faith but rather the fulfillment of it! From this beginning, the author advances a series of proofs of Jesus's supremacy over every rival. Hebrews 1 presents biblical texts showing that Christ is the Son of God who is greater than the angels. Jesus is greater than Moses—just as the owner of a house is greater than the house servant (3:1–6). Jesus is supreme over Joshua, who gave Israel rest only in the land of Canaan—whereas the true Savior gives the final rest of salvation glory (4:1–13). Studies of these rich chapters will yield treasures of biblical truth on the deity of Jesus and on his atoning work on the cross to save sinners.

Starting in chapter 5, the writer of Hebrews launches his comparison between Jesus, as the true High Priest of God's people, and the Levitical priests of the Old Testament. Hebrews 5–10 provides the most concentrated and enlightening teaching in the New Testament regarding the priestly work of our Savior and Lord. In the words of John Calvin, "There is, indeed, no book in Holy Scripture which speaks so clearly of the priesthood of Christ, which so highly exalts the virtue and dignity of that only true sacrifice which

He offered by His death . . . and, in a word, so fully explains that Christ is the end of the Law."[1]

When we see Jesus not only as the true messenger, the true prophet, and the true captain but also as the true priest and the true sacrifice by whom we are delivered from our sins, we embrace the writer's plea as summed up in Hebrews 10:23: "Let us hold fast the confession of our hope without wavering, for he who promised is faithful."

The author's **method** is to cite an Old Testament text that foretells the coming of the Messiah and then to show its fulfillment in Jesus and apply its message to the struggling hearts of his readers. One of his primary texts is Psalm 95, in which God warns against the danger of hardening one's heart and drifting from the gospel. By appealing to these Christ-centered Old Testament passages, Hebrews warns against the eternally dreadful results of forsaking Jesus, provides insight into the challenges that believers must face, and points out the importance of mutual exhortation among fellow Christians if they are to remain faithful. When you combine its forceful presentation of the supremacy of Christ with the author's persistent exhortations to his readers to endure in faith, together with the classic examples of faithfulness in "the Hall of Faith" of Hebrews 11 and the many searching applications in the final chapters, Hebrews is a uniquely valuable book of the New Testament that speaks powerfully to challenges that Christians face today.

Three perennial questions that are asked about Hebrews are relevant to our study of this text. First, *who wrote the book of Hebrews?* Since the **author** never identifies himself, theories and guesses have abounded. There are good reasons why the apostle Paul is the most common answer to this question, as was assumed by many in church history. For one thing, the contents of Hebrews sound Pauline, especially since the book alludes to one of Paul's favorite lines when it says, "my righteous one shall live by faith" (Heb. 10:38). Moreover, Hebrews 13:23 refers to Timothy—one of Paul's known protégés. On this basis, the writer must have had an association with Paul. Yet there are reasons why Paul is not likely to have written Hebrews. One telling sign is the style of the Greek writing in Hebrews, which follows a higher literary quality than the more common Greek of Paul's letters. Most conclusive is

1. John Calvin, *Hebrews and 1 & 2 Peter*, trans. William B. Johnston, Calvin's New Testament Commentaries 12 (Grand Rapids: Eerdmans, 1994), 1.

the statement of Hebrews 2:3, which says that the author's message "was attested to us by those who heard"—meaning that he himself was not an eye- or earwitness of Christ. Yet, in Galatians 1:12, Paul explicitly denies that he received the gospel secondhand and asserts that he received it directly from the Lord.

When Paul is removed from consideration, other authorial candidates abound. Suggestions include some of Paul's associates, such as Luke, Silas, Priscilla, Barnabas, and Apollos. In the end, we must agree with the ancient scholar Origen, who concluded, "Who wrote the epistle, in truth, God knows."[2] Indeed, since the Holy Spirit was pleased not to reveal the author of this book, we must content ourselves with knowing that it is the Word of God and was inspired through the pastoral concern of God's faithful human instrument.

Although we have described the spiritual challenge of the letter's recipients, another question is raised: *Were these Jewish Christians living in or near Rome or in Palestine?* Those who argue for a Palestinian **audience** point out the letter's doctrinal affinities with the Essene community near the Dead Sea. Against this view is the fact that, while this letter states that its recipients had not yet shed blood for their faith, such violent persecution had existed in and around Jerusalem since the beginning of the church. Recent scholarly consensus has shifted in the direction of Rome—in part because Clement of Rome, in a writing from around A.D. 95, showed familiarity with this letter. Moreover, the books of Romans and Acts describe a large Jewish church that had been in Rome from early on. Hebrews 13:24 adds, "Those who come from Italy send you greetings," which also supports Rome as the location of this struggling church. As for the letter's date, almost all scholars place it in the mid-60s, when persecution against Christians was rising in Rome, and before the destruction of Jerusalem's temple in the year 70—an event that would likely have been mentioned in Hebrews if it had already occurred.

Finally, *is Hebrews canonical—that is, should it be included among the New Testament books*? The early church's basic test for **canonicity** was proof of apostolicity. This did not mean that a book had to be written by an apostle, as is shown by the ready inclusion of Mark, Luke, and Acts. It was sufficient

2. Quoted in Eusebius, *Ecclesiastical History*, bk. 6, chap. 25, par. 14.

if the author was an associate of an apostle, as long as the book's teaching was apostolic in character. We should not think, however, that it was the church that created the canon—the reality is exactly the opposite. The canon—that is, the apostolic teaching of the New Testament message—created the church.

Hebrews seems to have been a later addition to the canon, since it is not listed in the first known roster of approved New Testament writings—the *Muratorian Fragment* (ca. 170–180). The most likely reason for this exclusion is that during these years of persecution it had not spread to all the churches. It did not take long, however, before the imprimatur of the Holy Spirit on this book, together with the sheer excellence of its contents, led God's people to recognize it. John Calvin, in the dedication to his commentary on the book, not only commends the church's acceptance of Hebrews but also hails its great value to those who study it with care and in faith: "Since the Epistle addressed to the Hebrews contains a full discussion of the eternal divinity of Christ, His supreme government, and only priesthood (which are the main points of heavenly wisdom), and as these things are so explained in it, that the whole power and work of Christ are set forth in the most graphic way, it rightly deserves to have the place and honor of an invaluable treasure in the Church."[3]

Richard D. Phillips
Coeditor of the Reformed Expository Commentary series
Coeditor of the Reformed Expository Bible Study series
Author of *Hebrews* (REC)

3. Calvin, *Hebrews and 1 & 2 Peter*, ix.

LESSON 1

A SUPERIOR LORD AND SAVIOR

Hebrews 1:1–14

THE BIG PICTURE

If one could summarize the book of Hebrews in just one word, it may well be the one that is used to describe Jesus in relation to the angels in 1:4—*superior*. Hebrews is a glorious exposition of the Old Testament Scriptures—one that makes manifest the absolute superiority of Jesus Christ above all and exhorts us to follow in the footsteps of all those who have placed their faith in him in the past. The author of Hebrews is unknown, though he almost certainly writes to predominantly Jewish believers who have placed their faith in Jesus Christ as the promised Messiah.

Hebrews 1, specifically, demonstrates Jesus's superiority over the angels of heaven—those glorious (yet still created) beings who dwell with God and serve his purposes. Jesus, the "radiance of the glory of God" (1:3), is distinct from even these angelic creatures—he holds the unique position of "begotten Son" of God (see 1:5). Not only did Jesus die to make purification for sinners, but he is also the one who will reign forever on the great throne of God (1:8). Jesus possesses an utterly unique relationship with the Father, who will ultimately deliver the nations to his gracious rule (1:12–13). The author of Hebrews grounds much of this argument in the words of the Old Testament Scriptures, which point toward Jesus as the Messiah—the promised King and Savior of all. This chapter soars with a declaration of the absolute supremacy and superiority of Jesus Christ—the Savior, King, and exalted Son of God. Even the angelic hosts, who serve the purposes of God, pale in comparison with the surpassing glory of this great Lord and Savior.

Read Hebrews 1:1–14.

GETTING STARTED

1. What struggles do you most often have with the Bible—in your personal devotions, in group study, or as you listen to preaching? What is most likely to undermine your confidence in the authority and sufficiency of Scripture?

2. How does your culture tend to downplay the significance or importance of Jesus Christ? What false and/or minimizing narratives about Jesus have you heard lately?

The Heart of Hebrews, pg. 6
This is what the book of Hebrews is about—the supremacy of Christ, along with the sufficiency of his work and the necessity of faith in him for salvation.

OBSERVING THE TEXT

3. With what subject does the author of Hebrews begin? Why might this be significant, particularly for the original audience of Jewish believers who received this epistle?

4. Look at the sheer amount of Old Testament Scripture that is quoted in this first chapter of Hebrews. What does this tell you about the perspective and intent of the author of this epistle?

5. In what ways does the author of Hebrews exalt Jesus throughout this first chapter? What titles does he give to him? What accomplishments are attributed to Jesus—both in the past and in the future?

UNDERSTANDING THE TEXT

6. How did God speak to his people throughout the age of the Old Testament, according to Hebrews 1:1? In what way has God spoken in "these last days," and how is this different from before (1:2)? What do we learn about God in just these opening two verses of Hebrews?

7. What claims are made about the divinity and supremacy of Jesus Christ in Hebrews 1:2–4? What does the author assert that Jesus has accomplished for God's people? Why might these claims about Jesus be so important to make at the outset of this epistle?

8. What might the author's mention of "angels" suggest about false teachings that may have circulated in the church when this letter was written (1:4)? Why might it be important to affirm that Jesus is exalted above the angels of heaven—even in our context today?

9. Why would the author of Hebrews choose the first two Old Testament references that he quotes in this chapter (Psalm 2:7 and 2 Samuel 7:14) to establish Jesus as being superior to angels (Heb. 1:5)? How are the angels commanded to respond to Jesus, and how does this further establish the author's point (1:6)?

A Perfect Revelation, pgs. 19–20

This passage exalts Christ not only as Lord of all but also as the one who perfectly reveals God in all his glory. He is the true king, but also the final prophet. . . . Without the Son we remain in the dark regarding the glory of God. But with the Son we have an ideal—indeed, a perfect—revelation of God.

10. What claims about Jesus does Hebrews 1:7–9 make, through the Old Testament references it applies to him? What special relationship does the author of Hebrews claim that Jesus possesses to God the Father, as he quotes in verses 10–12 from Psalm 102?

11. What is the ultimate future for Jesus the King, according to Hebrews 1:13? How does 1:14 offer a concluding distinction between Jesus and the angels, and why is this important? What is the role of angels, according to this final verse?

BIBLE CONNECTIONS

12. We have already been considering several Old Testament texts that are quoted throughout this first chapter of Hebrews. Turn now to Psalm 2 and read it in its entirety. How does this psalm establish Jesus as the great King of all nations? How is he distinguished from all human kings, and from angels as well, according to this psalm?

13. Read Colossians 1:15–20, which is sometimes called the "Christ Hymn" of Paul's letter to the Colossian church. What similarities do you see between the claims about Jesus that both Colossians 1 and Hebrews 1 make? What differences do you observe between them?

THEOLOGY CONNECTIONS

14. The Westminster Confession of Faith affirms that "God hath appointed a day wherein he will judge the world in righteousness by Jesus Christ, to whom all power and judgment is given of the Father" (33.1). How is this truth clearly taught and affirmed in Hebrews 1? Which Old Testament references does the chapter use to defend this teaching?

15. The heresy of Arianism, which ultimately taught that Jesus was a created being, was roundly condemned at the Council of Nicaea in A.D. 325. How might you use Hebrews 1 to counter the teaching that Jesus is a created being rather than the eternally existent God?

APPLYING THE TEXT

16. How can you seek to strengthen your trust in the final and authoritative Word of God that is contained in the Scriptures? What threatens your trust in God's Word?

17. What privileges do you possess, in Jesus Christ, as a child of God? How can this passage, which exalts him as supreme, remind you of the special place you have in the kingdom of God by faith?

18. What ought to be deeply comforting to you about the truths of this passage? How can the supremacy and sufficiency of Jesus protect you from despair, worry, and anxiety?

The Only Answer You Need, pg. 45

What is there you might need but that the risen and reigning Lord and Savior is the answer? There is nothing you might face, nothing you might lack, nothing you might need in all your weakness and sin and human frailty that is not found abundantly in him who loves you and gave himself for you and now reigns forever as Savior and Lord.

PRAYER PROMPT

Today, as you complete your study of this first chapter of the book of Hebrews, spend some time praising God for his clear, final, sufficient revelation. Thank him for the Bible, and ask him to enable you to see it as the gift it truly is. Pray that you would appreciate more deeply the beauty of God's revelation of himself in Jesus Christ, his Son. Then spend some time confessing the deficient views and perspectives that you are tempted to have concerning Jesus. Ask God to expand your understanding of Jesus's glory, supremacy, sufficiency, and eternal glorious reign, and pray that these truths would encourage you in the midst of suffering, hardship, and struggle.

LESSON 2

NOT DRIFTING FROM THE SUFFERING SAVIOR

Hebrews 2:1–18

THE BIG PICTURE

Hebrews 2 begins with stern words of warning—which come up often in this epistle. Followers of Jesus must not "drift" from what they have been taught about their Lord and Savior but must pay close attention to all they have heard. The author of Hebrews then reminds his readers of the glorious Savior whom they follow, contrasting him again with the angels of heaven and demonstrating the glorious eternal benefits that he offers to God's people. First, Jesus is the one who became—for a time—subjected to human life on earth (2:5–9). Psalm 8 paints a picture of the One who was made "lower than the angels" but who will one day be exalted above all things forever. Second, Jesus is the "founder of . . . salvation" who was made "perfect through suffering"—the crucified Savior who secured the redemption of God's people through his death on the cross (2:10; see also vv. 11–13). His close familial connection to God's people is striking—Jesus dies for those whom he calls "brothers"! Finally, Hebrews 2 reminds followers of Jesus that their Savior came to destroy Satan, sin, and death. Not only that, but his incarnation enables him to "help" God's people as they live for him in a fallen world—for he, too, was tempted (2:14–18). What a glorious picture of Jesus Christ! He descended to earth in humanity, submitted himself to suffering, and thus is able to help God's people in every way. Indeed, we must not drift from this Savior and this salvation.

Read Hebrews 2:1–18.

GETTING STARTED

1. In your experience, what are the usual factors that cause a person to "drift" from his or her faith in Jesus Christ? What gospel truths does such a person tend to forget—or deny—in the process?

2. How have you, or others around you, struggled with believing in the reality of a good God when great pain and suffering exist in this world? What false ideas about God can people embrace when they are faced with great suffering or immense temptation?

Don't Drift, pg. 55

"We must pay much closer attention to what we have heard," the writer of Hebrews exhorts, "lest we drift away from it." These words are as relevant today as when first written. We should fear to be separated from the anchor of God's Word, or to have any other hand on the wheel of our lives than the Captain of our salvation, who speaks in the Bible.

OBSERVING THE TEXT

3. How does Hebrews 2 continue with the theme of *angels* being compared with Jesus Christ? In what ways does it further contrast the life, ministry, and work of Jesus with the ministry and service of angels?

4. Look through this chapter, noting the privileged relationship that believers have with Jesus Christ, the Son of God. Why ought this to be an incredibly encouraging chapter?

5. What repeated words, phrases, or ideas does the author use in Hebrews 2? What Old Testament references does he cite, and why?

UNDERSTANDING THE TEXT

6. What is the warning that begins this chapter? What dangers are implied in this warning? What truths about the character of God are revealed in 2:1–4?

7. How does Hebrews 2:5–9 teach us about the incarnation of Jesus Christ? What is God the Father's ultimate purpose for Jesus Christ, the Son (2:9)? How might 2:8 help us to understand evil and suffering in our world today?

8. Hebrews 2:10 can be a difficult verse to understand. Does it imply that Jesus was not "perfect" before he suffered on the cross? If not, then what is this verse teaching about the suffering of Jesus—especially in relation to those whom he saves?

9. What familial language is attached to the people of God (2:11–13)? Why ought this to be deeply encouraging to followers of Jesus? How can this expand our understanding of our salvation and of the adoption that has caused God to be our Father?

Part of the Plan, pg. 57

Here, then, is the situation: Christ is presently reigning over his new kingdom and new humanity, yet at the same time the readers of this epistle, like us, find themselves still subject to the conditions of the old reality. . . . His use of the Old Testament demonstrates that what is happening now is part of God's predetermined and prerevealed plan for history.

10. In what ways is Jesus revealed to be our great "helper" in the final verses of this chapter (2:16–18)? Why might the author of Hebrews be introducing the "priestly" role of Jesus at this point in the epistle (2:17)?

11. What do we learn about Jesus's understanding of our human situation, suffering, and even temptation in 2:18? Why is the doctrine of the incarnation so important to a right understanding and application of this verse?

BIBLE CONNECTIONS

12. Psalm 8 is quoted in Hebrews 2:6–8; read that psalm in full now. In its original context, what does the psalmist seem to be writing about? How does the author of Hebrews apply this psalm? How might his application of the psalm inform your own study of the psalms with regard to their connections to Christ?

13. Read Romans 8:16–17, noting the title and privileges that the apostle Paul attaches to those who are in Christ. How is this language similar to the deeply encouraging language that is used of us in Hebrews 2?

THEOLOGY CONNECTIONS

14. Question 35 of the Heidelberg Catechism affirms this about the incarnation of Jesus Christ: "God's eternal Son, who is and continues true and eternal God, took upon Himself the very nature of man of the flesh and blood of the virgin Mary, by the operation of the Holy Spirit." How is this doctrine clearly explained in Hebrews 2:14–18? Why is this doctrine so important as we think about Jesus being our "help" during temptation?

15. John Calvin once wrote, "The promises, I say, are testimonies of divine grace. . . . In them [God] declares himself to be a father. . . . The promise, by which God adopts us to himself as his sons, holds the first place among them all. Now the cause and root of adoption is Christ."[1] How does the language of Hebrews 2 point us toward this glorious doctrine of our "adoption" into God's family through Jesus Christ? Why must we not neglect this way of thinking about our inclusion in God's family?

1. John Calvin, *Commentary on the Epistles of Paul to the Corinthians*, trans. William Pringle (repr., Bellingham, WA: Logos Bible Software, 2010), 2:137–38.

APPLYING THE TEXT

16. How ought this passage to help you understand the reality of evil, suffering, and temptation in this present world—even as you believe that Jesus is risen and reigning at the right hand of God?

17. What do you need to consider about your place in the family of God, given what you have studied in Hebrews 2? Why might we be tempted to forget to consider Jesus as our "brother" and God as our Father?

18. How might the truths about Jesus in this passage help you when you are in the midst of temptation? In what ways can you discipline yourself to remember the truths of Hebrews 2 and use them to strengthen yourself against sin, by the power of the Holy Spirit?

Jesus Did It All for You, pg. 82

All that God has done, in the redeeming work of Jesus Christ, was done not for angels but for you. It was *like you* that he became, and it was *for you* that he died. It is *with you* that he sympathizes now, knowing well your struggle. He is able—but are you willing?

PRAYER PROMPT

As you close your study of Hebrews 2 today, spend a few moments confessing to God your tendency to "drift" from so great a Savior—and from such a great salvation. Ask him to remind you of the immensity of his love for you in Christ, his Son. Pray that you would be freshly encouraged today by a Savior who took on flesh for you, died for you, and now lives to intercede for you and to help you when you are tempted. Ask God to help you pay close attention to all this as you grow in your love for your great Savior.

LESSON 3

SALVATION THROUGH THE GREATER MOSES

Hebrews 3:1–19

THE BIG PICTURE

Hebrews 3 continues a familiar theme: the superiority of both Jesus's person and his work for God's people. Now the author of Hebrews moves from making a contrast between Jesus and angels to making one between Jesus and Moses. Moses served as a faithful servant over the "house" of God during the wilderness days; Jesus carries the greater honor of sonship and is the *builder* of the new covenant "house" of God. In light of the fact that Jesus holds this exalted role, the author of Hebrews sternly warns his readers against falling away from faith in the exalted Savior. He quotes extensively from Psalm 95, which looks back at Korah's rebellion and the hardened hearts of the Israelites in the desert, and then adds his own words of warning against following in their footsteps. Faith in Jesus is thus about beginning well *and* finishing well; Christians are called to hold their "original confidence firm to the end" (3:14). If God's judgment could fall on his covenant people and prevent them from entering the land of his promised rest, then followers of Jesus today must steadfastly continue in faith, clinging to the greater Moses, who is their eternal and only hope.

Read Hebrews 3:1–19.

GETTING STARTED

1. What are some ways in which you've struggled to connect Moses and the Old Testament Law to Jesus and the Gospels and Epistles of the New Testament? Why can this be so difficult?

2. For Christians who believe in salvation by grace alone and through faith alone, why can Scripture passages full of "warning" be difficult to apply? If we believe that we are secure in our salvation, do we still need to be warned about falling away?

OBSERVING THE TEXT

3. How does this chapter, yet again, exalt Jesus as being greater and better than an Old Testament shadow? What superlatives are used to describe Jesus and his work?

Our Confidence, pg. 113

Of what are we to be confident? Not our own works or strength, but the power for salvation that is in Jesus Christ. It is our "original" confidence, namely, the very message of the gospel that saved us in the first place. This is what we need to persevere to the end.

4. What role does the Old Testament have in the argument of Hebrews 3? What passages does the author choose to use?

5. What does this chapter reveal to us about the character of God? What is frightening about the words of Hebrews 3?

UNDERSTANDING THE TEXT

6. This chapter begins with Jesus being contrasted not with angels but with Moses (3:1–6). How is Jesus different from and greater than Moses, in both his person and his work, according to these verses?

7. Why does the author use the language of a "house" throughout these verses? What might we learn about the Old Testament people of God through this language? What do we learn about Christ's role in relation to the church in these verses?

8. How does this chapter's warning against unbelief (3:7–12) flow naturally out of its presentation of Christ as being the greater Moses (3:1–6)? Why is Psalm 95:7–11 a helpful Old Testament reference as the author of Hebrews delivers this warning to his audience?

9. What words are used by the psalmist to describe the hearts of the rebellious Israelites as they disobeyed? What do you notice about the words that the author of Hebrews uses in his warning to his readers (3:12)? Why must Christians pay close attention to this warning?

10. What role do Christians have in the lives of their fellow believers, according to 3:13? How might this behavior serve to help others to hold their "original confidence" to the end (3:14)?

The Place Where God Reveals Himself, pg. 88

God is everywhere, yet he specially disclosed himself in a particular place, among his people in Israel, and especially at Jerusalem in the temple. . . . Today, if you want to learn about God, you should go to a church where his Word is taught. Though God is everywhere, it is still in his house where he especially reveals himself to those who come in faith.

11. What is effective about the author's use of consecutive questions in 3:16–18? What points does he seek to get across to his readers? Why and how are these points applicable to followers of Jesus today?

BIBLE CONNECTIONS

12. Skim through Numbers 16:1–40, which describes "Korah's rebellion" against God and against Moses. What sinful ways of thinking and acting led to this rebellion? Why might this have become an important lesson for God's people—even for hundreds of years afterward?

13. Read Philippians 1:3–6, noting especially the affirmation Paul makes in verse 6. Why is this comforting—especially as it relates to God's commitment to preserve the salvation of his people? Why is the truth of Philippians 1:6 not mutually exclusive with the appropriate warnings to Christians to endure that we find in passages such as Hebrews 3?

THEOLOGY CONNECTIONS

14. The fifth doctrine in the "doctrines of grace," which are sometimes referred to as the "five points" of Calvinism, is the doctrine of the

"perseverance of the saints." Reformed theology holds that believers' salvation is a work of God from beginning to end—that those who are truly redeemed cannot "lose" their salvation. Explain how Hebrews 3 is *not* a denial of this doctrine. How might biblical warnings actually be part of the way that God preserves his true saints?

15. John Calvin wrote of Jesus Christ, "He is the sovereign lawgiver Moses, writing his law on the tables of our hearts by his Spirit."[1] How does this teaching connect to all the comparisons that the author of Hebrews makes between Moses and Jesus in this chapter? How does Calvin's description explain the supremacy of Jesus's work for God's people over Moses's?

APPLYING THE TEXT

16. How do the first six verses of this passage help you to better understand the role of Moses, the Old Testament Law, and the people of God, as we see these things in the Old Testament? Why is this important for you as a student of the Bible?

1. John Calvin, "Preface to Olivétan's New Testament," in *Calvin: Commentaries*, ed. Joseph Haroutunian, Library of Christian Classics 23 (Philadelphia: Westminster Press, 1958), 69.

17. What warnings from this passage did you find particularly convicting, frightening, or startling? How can you respond rightly to such warnings?

18. How can you play a greater role in encouraging and exhorting your brothers and sisters in Christ toward faithfulness and endurance, in the spirit of Hebrews 3:13? What might that look like practically?

PRAYER PROMPT

You are concluding a study of a chapter that is full of stern warnings—warnings against unbelief, stubbornness, and faithlessness. Today, pray that God would keep you holding fast to your original confidence—your trust in the finished work of Jesus Christ on your behalf. Ask him to use the witness of Scripture—Hebrews 3, Psalm 95, and the Old Testament accounts of the Israelites' sin in the wilderness—to remind you of your need to cling to faith in Jesus. Ask him for help, by the power of the Holy Spirit, to understand the work of Jesus on your behalf, to reject sinful rebellion and disobedience, and to finish by faith just as you began by faith.

How Do We Survive This Wilderness? pg. 103

Will we make it through this desert life safe across Jordan to the Promised Land ahead? We will if we trust ourselves to Jesus, relying on the strength he gives to all his pilgrim people. He is the shepherd of his flock.

LESSON 4

RESTING IN OUR GREAT HIGH PRIEST

Hebrews 4:1–5:10

THE BIG PICTURE

As Hebrews 4 begins, we realize that the author of the book is both concluding the discussion of chapter 3 and also moving us forward toward yet another magnificent view of the supremacy and sufficiency of our Savior, Jesus Christ. Jesus has already been held up as being great and as being worthier than Moses (3:1–6); now he is exalted as the Great High Priest who, in a way far greater than Joshua did, invites us into the restful presence of God himself (4:14–16). All throughout the wilderness wanderings of the people of God in the Old Testament, the promise of entering the "rest" of the land had been held out to them. While Joshua ultimately led them into the land, it became clear that this was not the final and ultimate "rest" of God (4:8–10). There is only one way for sinful people to find final rest in the presence of God: they must enter through the "source of eternal salvation"—the blood of Jesus Christ (5:9). It is Jesus Christ—one who is greater than both Moses and Joshua—who can deal gently with sinners as their Great High Priest and make a perfect appeal to God the Father on their behalf. The good news is that Jesus's priesthood, like that of Melchizedek, is perpetual; he alone obtains eternal rest for sinners who put their trust in him.

Read Hebrews 4:1–5:10.

GETTING STARTED

1. What are some of the ways in which people tend to talk about "rest"? Why do some people, in your experience, struggle with a general sense of *restlessness*? How might understanding the gospel as the path to ultimate, eternal "rest" be helpful?

2. What cultural connotations are associated with the concept of "priesthood"? Have you found considering Jesus as the "High Priest" to be helpful, encouraging, confusing, or challenging? Why?

OBSERVING THE TEXT

3. As chapter 4 opens, how is it apparent that the author of Hebrews is continuing his discussion from chapter 3? What Old Testament passage is again quoted?

The Promise of Entering God's Rest, pg. 122

What a difference it makes to rest upon the Lord Jesus and thereby to enter God's rest. This brings peace with God and produces inward joy. That is all the more reason to trust in the Lord during this present day of opportunity, when the promise of entering God's rest still stands.

4. Why might the theme of rest be so central throughout chapter 4? How is rest connected to the character and actions of God?

5. In what new ways does the author of Hebrews talk about Jesus? What metaphors does he use? What actions does Jesus accomplish for God's people?

UNDERSTANDING THE TEXT

6. How do the opening verses of Hebrews 4 make it clear that the concept of entering God's rest was always broader than the prospect of entering the promised land (4:1–5)? What, then, does it ultimately mean to enter God's rest?

7. How do Hebrews 4:6–7 and 11 function as both a warning and an invitation? What is so appealing about this gracious invitation, according to 4:8–10? How does this inform our understanding of salvation by grace through faith?

8. What key doctrines about the Word of God are affirmed in 4:12–13? How do these verses connect to the surrounding context of this letter and flow out of what has been discussed before?

9. How is the great high priesthood of Jesus explained to us in Hebrews 4:14–16? In what ways does Jesus serve as our priest? What does he accomplish on our behalf? With what attitude can we now approach the throne of God the Father?

10. In what ways is Jesus similar to high priests from Israel who went before him (5:1–4)? How is he different and set apart as being a greater High Priest (5:5–6)?

The Word Comes Alive within You, pg. 136

Through his Word God himself teaches us, rebukes and corrects us, trains us in righteousness and equips us for every good work. When you come to God's Word in faith—when you open up your heart and mind to the teachings of the Bible, either as it is preached or in your own reading of it—that Word comes alive within you because it is sent by God himself for that purpose.

11. What does the author of Hebrews explain about the suffering that Jesus underwent as our High Priest (5:7–8)? What is the ultimate result for God's people of the suffering of our Great High Priest (5:9)? Why is the mention of "Melchizedek" significant to an understanding of Christ's priesthood for God's people (5:10)?

BIBLE CONNECTIONS

12. Skim through Judges 1, paying particular attention to verses 27–36. How might the Israelites' failure to utterly complete the conquest of the land of Canaan following Joshua's death be a hint that there must have been a greater, more ultimate rest still to come? What happened as a result of their incomplete conquest of Canaan?

13. Read Genesis 14:17–20—the passage of Scripture in which Melchizedek is first introduced to us. While the author of Hebrews will come back to Melchizedek, consider for now the significance of the fact that his priesthood is linked with Jesus. Why is this? In what way is this priestly figure from Genesis 14 pointing forward to the Great High Priest of God's people?

THEOLOGY CONNECTIONS

14. The Westminster Confession of Faith gives these instructions concerning the Sabbath Day: "This Sabbath is then kept holy unto the Lord, when men, after a due preparing of their hearts, and ordering of their common affairs beforehand, do not only observe an holy rest, all the day, from their own works, words, and thoughts about their worldly employments and recreations, but also are taken up, the whole time, in the public and private exercises of his worship, and in the duties of necessity and mercy" (21.8). How did God's gift of the Sabbath Day (which is now often called the "Lord's Day") teach God's people about his ultimate rest—both under the old covenant and under the new covenant today?

15. Martin Luther, contrasting the priesthood of Jesus with the priesthood of the Old Testament, writes, "But with the priesthood of Christ is true spiritual remission, sanctification and absolution. These avail before God—God grant that it be true of us—whether we be outwardly excommunicated, or holy, or not. Christ's blood has obtained for us pardon forever acceptable with God."[1] How should these realities about Christ's work, along with the truths of the passage that you have just studied, strengthen your faith and assurance?

1. Martin Luther, "Christ Our Great High Priest," ed. Shane Rosenthal, available online from Christian Classics Ethereal Library, accessed February 12, 2020, https://ccel.org/ccel/luther/sermons.iii.html.

APPLYING THE TEXT

16. How ought this passage to serve as a warning, to all who read it, about the importance of entering the rest of God? Why should the truths of this passage stir your heart toward more evangelism and witness for Jesus Christ?

17. What ought Hebrews 4:12–13 to teach you about your use of God's Word in your own life? In the lives of others? What can you expect to happen as God's Word is spoken, taught, read, and shared?

18. How should viewing Jesus Christ as your Great High Priest strengthen your assurance of your salvation? How might you pray to God in a way that is more informed by this glorious reality?

A Priest Who Ministers for Us, pg. 162

The answer . . . to our need of assurance, is the appointment of Jesus Christ as our High Priest. He has already completed the work of dying for our sins. He has gone into heaven to offer his sacrificial blood for our sake. There he now sits enthroned as a priest who ministers on our behalf, praying for us, interceding with the Father, and sending the heavenly manna needed to feed and tend our faith.

PRAYER PROMPT

This passage holds out to us a glorious reality: that we will share in the eternal rest of God himself. It comes with a warning, which we dare not reject. But it also comes with great grace, for there is still time for us to repent and trust the Great High Priest, who alone can open the door to the very throne room of God through his sacrifice for sins. Today, as you close your study of God's Word, praise God for his promise that we will share in his eternal rest. Ask him to help you to trust Jesus, your Great High Priest, who has gone before you and is patient with you in your weakness and struggle. Then ask God for the boldness to share this warning and gracious invitation with those who have not yet put their faith in Jesus . . . for there is still time!

LESSON 5

HOLDING FAST TO THE CERTAIN PROMISE

Hebrews 5:11–6:20

THE BIG PICTURE

As Hebrews 5 draws to a close, the book's author again makes use of some very specific words of rebuke and instruction for his readers, as he calls them toward more spiritual maturity (5:11–6:3). He characterizes them as infants in the faith who still need to be fed with "milk" instead of "solid food." They are not yet where they ought to be in terms of their mature understanding and application of the gospel of Jesus Christ. This rebuke gives way to an extremely sobering warning: if those who have "tasted" the goodness of God and had some understanding of the gospel within the context of the church were to fall away, their apostasy would be irreversible (6:4–8). These verses contain a serious warning about sharing in the privileges of the people of God, only to ultimately reject the Son of God. Finally, though, our passage concludes with encouraging—and confident—words of exhortation for believers in Jesus to endure until the end (6:9–20). The author of Hebrews affirms his own confidence in their ultimate endurance, given the evidence of real Christian fruit that they display. But, more than that, his confidence that they will endure comes from the promise of God himself, who kept his promises to Abraham and eternally anchors the promises that he makes to his people in his Son, who has gone "behind the curtain" (6:19) to earn salvation on our behalf (6:19–20).

Read Hebrews 5:11–6:20.

GETTING STARTED

1. How have you struggled with the motivation to keep on growing in your faith—and particularly in your understanding and grasp of Christian doctrine and theology? Why is it important for believers in Jesus to keep growing in their understanding of the faith, even after their conversion?

2. Why can it be so damaging and confusing, for both churches and individual Christians, when well-known Christian leaders appear to "fall away" from their faith? How have you seen this raise serious questions and even shake Christians' faith?

Perseverance to the End, pg. 183

The single-minded aim of the writer of Hebrews all through this epistle has been that through faith in Jesus Christ we must persevere until the end. . . . That is his great desire, to lead his readers into a mature understanding of Jesus Christ and his saving work so that their faith may endure to the end.

OBSERVING THE TEXT

3. As this passage begins, how is it immediately evident that the author of Hebrews has gotten a bit more personal in his application and instruction? How would you describe his tone as Hebrews 5 concludes?

4. What questions are raised in this passage? What particular doctrinal issues and debates might arise from a study of this section of Hebrews?

5. How does this passage ultimately conclude? What is the ultimate source of our confidence that Christians will faithfully endure until the end?

UNDERSTANDING THE TEXT

6. How does the author of Hebrews describe the current state of his audience's faith (5:11–14)? What is the main metaphor that he uses to describe them? How might this be helpful, and perhaps even a bit unsettling (and intentionally so), for his audience?

7. In what ways does the author of Hebrews want his audience to grow toward maturity, according to 6:1–3? What kind of "solid food" might he have in mind, when it comes to their growth in faith and understanding?

8. What kind of people does Hebrews 6:4–8 seem to describe? In what sense have they had a share in Christianity? What privileges have they enjoyed? Why is their turning away particularly damaging and egregious?

9. What good fruit and evidence of true faith does the author of Hebrews mention (6:9–12)? How does he exhort his readers to continue? What does he use to motivate them to diligently persevere in their faith?

Impossible to Restore, pg. 191

This is who these people are, those who have a personal but nonetheless secondary or indirect experience of Christianity. They may serve, they may preach, they may handle the powers of the age to come, but they are not really Christ's own. About such people the following assertion is made: "It is impossible to restore [them] . . . if they then fall away."

10. What is encouraging about the way this passage concludes (6:13–20)? How does the author of Hebrews intend for Abraham's example of waiting on the promise of God to encourage his audience in their endurance and perseverance in faith?

11. What role does Jesus Christ have in securing the promises of God on behalf of God's people (6:19–20)? What images does the author of Hebrews provide to help his audience to picture the work of Jesus Christ as a sure and steady anchor for their souls?

BIBLE CONNECTIONS

12. As he points his readers to the sure promise of God, the author of Hebrews calls them to look back at Abraham, who put his faith in God's promises over the course of many years and throughout much testing. Read Genesis 22:11–17, from which the author of Hebrews quotes in the passage you have studied. How did God show himself to be faithful to Abraham? How was Abraham called to trust in God's promises?

13. Read Philippians 3:12–14. How does the apostle Paul model the continuous pursuit of growth in Christ and of eternal life—even by one

who is already spiritually mature? How might you better live out this godly discontent as you seek to grow more and more in grace?

THEOLOGY CONNECTIONS

14. The Heidelberg Catechism states in answer 53 that the Christian can affirm that the Spirit "is also given me, to make me by a true faith partaker of Christ and all His benefits, to comfort me, and to abide with me forever." How does this statement support the Reformed doctrine of the "perseverance of the saints"? Explain how this statement does not conflict with Hebrews 6:4–8.

15. The great Reformer John Calvin encouraged believers with these words: "No one can travel so far that he does not make some progress each day. So let us never give up. Then we shall move forward daily in the Lord's way. And let us never despair because of our limited success. Even though it is so much less than we would like, our labor is not wasted when today is better than yesterday!" (*Institutes*, 3.6.5). How is this similar to the exhortations that the author of Hebrews makes in the passage you have just studied?

APPLYING THE TEXT

16. How might you use Hebrews 5:11–6:3 to respond to people who suggest that studying theology is a waste of time? Why might these verses be a needed rebuke to some people who are in the church even today?

17. What warning can this passage (and particularly 6:4–8) provide to those who are involved in the church and are doing lots of Christian activities . . . and who see those things as evidence that they are truly Christians? How does this passage introduce us to a frightening new category of people who "taste" the things of God without ever truly putting their faith in Jesus?

18. How can you more diligently "anchor" your hope in Jesus this week? What truths about his work on your behalf does this passage call you to more actively remember?

Anchored in Heaven, pg. 216

Unlike the hope of the world, which goes nowhere and has no anchor, our hope in Christ goes before us into heaven, where it is anchored in the unchanging character of God and the oath he has sworn. Our hope goes where we cannot yet go ourselves. It goes into heaven, where Christ is now.

PRAYER PROMPT

As we close our study of Hebrews 5:11–6:20, we look back on yet another passage that is full of rebuke, warning, and encouragement. Today, spend some time praying in response to each of these emphases. First, ask God to give you the motivation and desire to continue to grow in your understanding of his Word, of Christian doctrine, and of theology. Second, pray that he would protect you from the danger of "tasting" and "sharing" in Christian community and teaching without the reality of true repentance and faith taking place in your heart. Third, beg God to help you to anchor your ultimate hope for endurance in his ultimate promise of salvation and perseverance.

LESSON 6

AFTER THE ORDER OF MELCHIZEDEK

Hebrews 7:1–28

THE BIG PICTURE

As you will notice, there is one main Old Testament figure with whom Hebrews 7 compares and contrasts Jesus: Melchizedek. The author of Hebrews takes a deep dive into the strange encounter that Abraham has with this "high priest," recounting the priestly ministry of this mysterious figure as well as the honor and respect that is shown to him by Abraham. While we know almost nothing about Melchizedek other than that he served as both "priest of God" and "king of Salem" in ancient Canaan, the author of Hebrews wants us to notice his *lack* of lineage—we are told about neither his ancestors nor his death nor the end of his priestly ministry (7:3). Melchizedek therefore stands out as one who holds a kind of archetypal priestly and kingly ministry in perpetuity—an Old Testament symbol of an unending and permanent religious and political reign. This, according to the author of Hebrews, points forward to the eternal, heavenly, and ultimate high priesthood of Jesus Christ. Long before the establishment of the Levitical priesthood, which was imperfect, God had given his people a glimpse of an eternal royal priestly ministry through this mysterious interaction between Abraham and Melchizedek. Jesus is the Son of God—the "holy, innocent, unstained" Priest (7:26) and the great King (7:25) for God's people, who is "able to save to the uttermost" sinners who will repent and turn to him.

Read Hebrews 7:1–28.

GETTING STARTED

1. Why can comparison be such a useful teaching tool—even across multiple subjects? How has comparison, particularly between Jesus and Old Testament concepts and characters, been helpful to you in your growing understanding of the gospel?

2. What are some questions that you have had in the past about the Levitical priesthood of the Old Testament? Can you think of some hints that were "built in" to the Levitical sacrificial system that indicated that something more was to come for the people of God?

Peace with Our Melchizedek, pg. 230
Jesus is our Melchizedek. He is our King of Righteousness, cleansing us from our sin by his blood and clothing us in the royal robes of his perfect obedience. That is why his is the city of peace, where those who find righteousness in him shall dwell forever in peace with him.

OBSERVING THE TEXT

3. How does the main character, as well as the main subject, of Hebrews 7 become immediately apparent as the passage begins? Where have we heard this Old Testament character being mentioned before in this epistle?

4. What Old Testament passages does the author of Hebrews quote in this chapter? Why does he select these passages? What points is he seeking to make to his readers?

5. How does this chapter, overall, add to our expanding view of the supremacy and sufficiency of the person and work of Jesus Christ?

UNDERSTANDING THE TEXT

6. Hebrews 7 begins by introducing Melchizedek, because the author has just mentioned that Jesus's priesthood is "after the order" of this Melchizedek (6:20). What needs to be explained about Melchizedek in relation to Jesus in this chapter? What dual roles did Melchizedek hold, and how do they relate to Jesus?

7. What primary characteristics about Melchizedek does the author want the readers to notice (7:1–10)? What is noteworthy about Abraham's treatment of him? What is interesting about his lineage?

8. What does Jesus's priesthood being "after the order" of Melchizedek imply about the Levitical priesthood (7:11)? What is significant about the tribe into which Jesus is born, as it relates to his role as priest (7:14)?

9. If Jesus becomes a priest in a manner that is similar to Melchizedek but *not* on the basis of his tribal association, why is this tremendously good news (7:15–19)? What does this mean for the permanence and effectiveness of his work on behalf of God's people?

The Final Priesthood, pgs. 239–40

When we think of Jesus as high priest, many of us think only of him fulfilling the ministry of Aaron and the Levites. We think of Christ offering his perfect righteousness and precious blood to atone for our sins. . . . Yet this was not the final priesthood; the priesthood typified by Aaron has given way to that of Melchizedek.

10. What prevented the Levitical priests from serving as the final and perpetual answer for God's sinful people (7:23)? How and why is a *risen* Christ able to serve as a priest in a permanent way (7:24–25)?

11. What truths about the character of Jesus are we reminded of as the chapter closes (7:26–28)? Why is the sinlessness of Jesus so important for our understanding of the doctrine of justification, the doctrine of intercession, and the incarnation?

BIBLE CONNECTIONS

12. Today, read Psalm 110, in which David considers the kingly priesthood of Melchizedek and looks forward to the coming of One who will be even greater than him. How do David's words anticipate the teaching and explanation of Hebrews 7 regarding Jesus Christ?

13. Read Romans 3:21–26—one of the richest explanations of Jesus's work on the cross for sinners. How does the apostle Paul further explain the sacrificial and priestly role that Jesus took in justly providing salvation for sinners in the sight of God the Father?

THEOLOGY CONNECTIONS

14. The Westminster Confession of Faith declares, "It pleased God, in his eternal purpose, to choose and ordain the Lord Jesus, his only begotten Son, to be the Mediator between God and man; the Prophet, Priest and King; the Head and Savior of his Church" (8.1). How is this truth affirmed in Hebrews 7? How are these multiple roles of Jesus Christ foreshadowed in the person and work of Melchizedek in Genesis 14?

15. Why is the doctrine of the physical, bodily resurrection of Jesus Christ so important to our understanding of his eternal priesthood for God's people (see Heb. 7:16, 23)?

APPLYING THE TEXT

16. How ought your study of Hebrews 7 to encourage you in your careful study of the Old Testament? In what ways can this passage remind you to read and study all of Scripture in light of the life and work of Jesus Christ?

17. What part of Hebrews 7 is most personally encouraging to you as you consider your relationship with Jesus Christ? How do the truths in this passage cause you to admire and treasure your Savior even more?

18. How should the eternal priestly role of Jesus strengthen your assurance of salvation and enable you to push back against doubt, fear, and anxiety regarding your favor with God?

PRAYER PROMPT

As you close your study of Hebrews 7, begin by asking God to grow your understanding and appreciation of the Old Testament. Thank him for the way that even somewhat obscure figures, such as Melchizedek, paved the way for the glorious ministry of Jesus Christ—our great Priest and King. Then pray that God would continue to grow and expand your love for Jesus and your understanding of his eternal priestly work on your behalf. Praise him that you have a priest who lives forever and can intercede for you—One who is able to save you to the uttermost!

The Ultimate Priest, pg. 263
Jesus Christ is the one to whom all the priests beforehand pointed: the one who is holy, blameless, and pure; the one who is qualified to sacrifice "once for all" with the offering of his own blood; the one who is able to redeem us from sin and reconcile us to God.

LESSON 7

A BETTER COVENANT

Hebrews 8:1–9:14

THE BIG PICTURE

As we move on from considering the priestly and kingly ministry of Jesus in light of the Old Testament figure of Melchizedek, the author of Hebrews now invites us to consider the Levitical priesthood once more—as well as all of the old covenant regulations for worship, sacrifice, and entrance into the Holy Place of God. Jesus Christ is the substance of which all the old covenant regulations were mere "copies" and "shadows" (see 8:1–7). The author then quotes extensively from Jeremiah 31 and argues that the old covenant was incomplete—that it lacked an ultimate fulfillment, which, when it arrived in the work of Jesus Christ, rendered that covenant obsolete (8:8–13). As Hebrews 9 opens, the readers are reminded of the incredible amount of detail, regulations, and preparations that were involved in old covenant worship in the "Holy Place"—all of which are used by the Holy Spirit to indicate that the ultimate way for God's people to enter into his presence is yet to come, through Jesus (9:1–10). We end this passage by coming to the final revelation of Jesus Christ, who secures an "eternal redemption" for God's people through his entrance into the Holy Place by his own blood (9:12; see also vv. 13–14). Here is a passage, then, full of rich encouragement for New Testament believers. Jesus Christ, our Savior, is the substance to which all of the Old Testament rituals, sacrifices, and worship preparations pointed. Through his blood, we can enter into the very presence of God.

Read Hebrews 8:1–9:14.

GETTING STARTED

1. What misunderstandings about the Old Testament law and sacrificial system have you personally held? What confusing or mistaken views have you heard, or been taught, in the past?

2. So far, in your study of Hebrews, how have you observed the way that a deepening understanding of the Old Testament can enrich your understanding of and appreciation for Jesus Christ and his salvation?

Better Promises, pg. 274

Jesus's ministry is superior because his covenant is superior, having better promises. . . . It is superior because Jesus is superior, because his work actually saves us. . . . He wins our salvation by his perfect and finished work, a work so finished that he sat down.

OBSERVING THE TEXT

3. How does the author of Hebrews use the Old Testament (its quotations, themes, and pictures) throughout this passage? What particular passages does he choose to quote, and why?

4. What misunderstandings—particularly those held by Jewish believers in Jesus Christ—might the author of Hebrews be seeking to correct throughout this passage?

5. How would you summarize the function that the Old Testament rules, regulations, and rituals played in the lives of Old Testament believers? Why is it helpful for believers in Jesus today to understand at least some of the details of the Levitical and sacrificial system?

UNDERSTANDING THE TEXT

6. What is it about the priestly ministry of Jesus that makes it so superior to the Levitical priesthood, according to Hebrews 8:1–6? What does he accomplish for God's people? What is utterly unique about his role and his position?

7. How should we rightly understand the Old Testament priestly ministry, sacrifices, and ritual laws, according to these first six verses?

8. What is the author's purpose in quoting so extensively from Jeremiah 31 (Heb. 8:8–12)? How does he conclude the point that he is making (8:13)? What ought this to teach us about the old covenant in relation to the new covenant that comes through Jesus Christ?

God Bestows What He Desires, pg. 285

This is what God desires: an expression of fidelity, of marital commitment and intimacy, the loving cry of the faithful wife: "I know him—he is my Lord." What God desires from us, what he requires from us, he bestows upon us by grace in this new and better covenant.

9. Why does the author of Hebrews explain the regulations and practices of the earthly Holy Place in such detail (9:1–7)? What do you notice about the details he chooses to include?

10. What were the specific regulations regarding the Holy Place communicating to God's people (9:8–10)? Who was communicating these truths to them (9:8)? Why is this significant for our own understanding of the Old Testament as well as our understanding of the Holy Spirit?

11. How does the work of Jesus Christ perfect the Old Testament rituals of sacrifice (9:11–12)? Why is his work eternally efficacious, as opposed to the shed blood of animals? What is the result of Jesus's work for those who repent and believe in him (9:13–14)?

BIBLE CONNECTIONS

12. Look back to Jeremiah 31:31–34 and read the prophet's words about God's "new covenant" with his people. How are these promises so

gloriously fulfilled in Jesus? How will they be perfected even more fully when we are in the presence of Jesus after death?

13. Read 1 John 1:9, which contains a very simple and straightforward promise. Why is God's Word able to make this promise, based on what you have studied in these chapters of Hebrews?

THEOLOGY CONNECTIONS

14. Hebrews 9:14 describes believers using words that are linked to priesthood—we "serve" the living God. One key concept of the Reformation during the sixteenth century was the "priesthood of all believers"—the biblical idea that every believer has access to God through Jesus Christ and by the power of the Holy Spirit. Why is this an important biblical idea? What dangers does this teaching help to avoid?

15. Chapter 18.1 of the Westminster Confession of Faith asserts that believers in Jesus can "be certainly assured that they are in the state of grace." How, and why, is such assurance possible, based on what you have just studied in Hebrews 8 and 9?

APPLYING THE TEXT

16. How might our study and understanding of the Old Testament rituals and preparations for worship guide our approach to worship now, even in this era of the new covenant? In what ways might you need to be called toward a deeper attitude of awe and reverence for God?

17. What effect has your study of this passage in Hebrews had on your understanding of the wonder, cost, and depth of your own salvation?

18. How should this passage—and particularly Hebrews 9:11–14—increase the confidence with which you approach God as your Father in both prayer and worship? How do the truths about the blood and sacrifice of Christ inspire you to obey and serve God?

To Be His Vessel, pg. 308

Once "purified," we are "to serve the living God." To serve God is to be his vessel, to have him pour himself into us for the shining of his glory into the world, both now and forever. . . . But of course none of this is possible until we have first been cleansed by the blood of Jesus Christ—the precious blood of the Son of God that is superior to that of bulls and goats.

PRAYER PROMPT

The passage that we have just studied is one that calls us to look back—to understand the rituals, preparations, and regulations of Old Testament worship. Pray that God would enable you to see the tremendous weight of worship as well as the privilege that it is to enter into his presence! But this passage also calls you to consider all that you have now, through faith in Jesus Christ. Your Savior accomplished and fulfilled the realities to which the old covenant rituals all pointed when he entered into the ultimate "Holy Place" on your behalf through his blood. As you conclude today, praise God for his marvelous grace and ask him to strengthen you for obedience and service for his glory.

LESSON 8

ONE FINAL SACRIFICE

Hebrews 9:15–10:18

THE BIG PICTURE

The author of Hebrews, intent on continuing to expand his readers' understanding of the superiority and sufficiency of Jesus Christ as Savior, turns back yet again to some Old Testament concepts and pictures. Under the old covenant, God's people were sprinkled with blood, which indicated their responsibility to keep God's law—under threat of death (9:15–22). God was teaching them that sin against him demanded the shedding of blood (9:22). The marvelous hope of the gospel is that Jesus has entered "once for all" into the presence of God to make a final and efficacious sacrifice for God's people through his own blood (9:23–28). Unlike the repeated sacrifices of the Old Testament—which reminded God's people of the need for forgiveness but never finally took away sin—Jesus Christ comes with his own "body," according to the will of God, in order to bring true holiness and forgiveness to God's people (10:1–10). All of this means that Jesus's sacrifice for God's people is a final sacrifice—he has fully accomplished salvation for those who believe in him and is now "seated" at the right hand of God waiting for the final and visible victory over all his enemies (10:11–18). God's people need no further sacrifice—the days of the new covenant have come, and the Savior will soon return as King and Judge.

Read Hebrews 9:15–10:18.

GETTING STARTED

1. When you realize that you have sinned, how do you tend to react? What biblical truths do you tend to remember? What truths do you tend to forget?

2. How do you picture Jesus right now? Where is he, according to Scripture, and what is he doing? Why ought this to be encouraging to you in your daily walk with God?

OBSERVING THE TEXT

3. What familiar themes did you notice the author discussing during your initial reading of this passage? How are these themes and ideas further developed in this passage?

The Only Payment for Sin, pg. 317
Let us get this into our heads, that once we have sinned against God there is no way for the sin to be put away, except by the shedding of blood. But the price for our redemption is one that we cannot pay ourselves and yet survive. What we need is someone to pay it for us, a substitute, in whom is the power of eternal life.

4. What words, images, or concepts are repeated throughout Hebrews 9:15–10:18? How would you summarize the way that the author describes Jesus Christ throughout this passage?

5. What Old Testament passages does the author reference in 9:15–10:18? Why might he have chosen to include these particular verses and references?

UNDERSTANDING THE TEXT

6. What is helpful about the picture of a "will" that Hebrews 9:16–17 introduces? How does this metaphor enable us to better understand our eternal inheritance as well as the manner by which it was secured?

7. Why was *blood* such an important part of the old covenant system, according to the author of Hebrews? What was God seeking to teach his people, through blood, about sin, forgiveness, and purity (9:22)?

8. What is familiar about the language that the author of Hebrews uses to describe the Old Testament sacrificial system (9:23–24)? Why is it important that the Levitical system contained "copies" of true, heavenly realities? How do they point to the real work of justification and salvation that Jesus performed, according to 9:24–26?

9. What does the author of Hebrews explain, quite explicitly, about the insufficiency of the Old Testament sacrificial system (10:1–4)? What truths did the ongoing sacrifices reveal to God's people in the Old Testament? What is the significance of the *body* of Jesus Christ in the fulfillment of God's will and in our salvation (10:5, 10)?

10. What distinguished the sacrifice of Jesus from all the sacrifices that had come before, under the old covenant system (10:11–14)? What does this mean for God's people, who receive the blessings of Jesus's sacrifice? What did Jesus do after his sacrifice, and why is this so significant?

Not Our Own Merits, pg. 341

All of this is why Jesus did not need any animal sacrifices when he appeared in the true sanctuary that is heaven. He had done God's will and he entered on his own merits. This, of course, is something we cannot say about ourselves. We do not enter on our own merits, but on his merits, his blood having washed away our sin.

11. How is the promise of the new covenant tied to the hope of ultimate forgiveness (10:15–17)? Why might the author of Hebrews be returning at this point to this passage from Jeremiah 31, which he has quoted earlier in the letter?

BIBLE CONNECTIONS

12. Take a moment to read Exodus 24:6–8—a passage that describes the ratifying of the covenant by Moses and the people of God. What do the people of God promise to do? What does the thrown blood represent, with regard to their promise? How does this passage explain the need for the better blood of Jesus Christ to be shed for the sins of God's people?

13. In John 19:30, Jesus lifts up his voice as he dies on the cross and exclaims, "It is finished." How has your study of this passage from Hebrews expanded your understanding of that cry that Jesus made? What, exactly, has been finished?

THEOLOGY CONNECTIONS

14. The answer to question 5 of the Heidelberg Catechism, which asks us if we are able to live up to the law of God, is this: "No . . . I am prone by

nature to hate God and my neighbor." What theological doctrines does the answer to this catechism question reflect? How does this answer shed light on the passage from Exodus 24 that you read earlier, as well as on the ultimate need for a Savior?

15. We often rightly think about sanctification as being an ongoing process, as believers in Jesus become more and more like their Savior. Hebrews 10:14, though, declares that Jesus "has perfected for all time those who are being sanctified." How does this verse call us to see sanctification as an already-but-not-yet reality in the lives of Christians? Explain this tension that exists in the Christian life, as best you can.

APPLYING THE TEXT

16. How might this passage from the book of Hebrews enable you to better explain the Old Testament law and sacrificial system to a new believer? How did the Levitical priesthood serve God's people in the Old Testament? How did it point forward to Jesus?

Made Perfect, pg. 347
Christ was made perfect in his role as Savior and High Priest for the church in order to sit at God's right hand . . . so that we would be made perfect in him for our role as worshiping priests in heaven.

17. What truths about God that you encountered during your study of this passage are most encouraging to you personally?

18. How should the image of Jesus being seated "at the right hand of God" (10:12) strengthen your faith today? Why should this image also encourage you to obey and serve God?

PRAYER PROMPT

As you close your time of studying yet another theologically rich passage from the book of Hebrews, begin by thanking God for his faithful revelation to his people throughout history. Praise him for the gift of the law, which taught his people about his holy character and the need for sacrifices to cover their sins. Then praise him for the great fulfillment of all to which the law pointed—thank him that the "copies" of heavenly things pointed forward to the truly efficacious blood of Jesus Christ. Thank him that Jesus, his Son, provided a once-for-all sacrifice for your sins. Finally, ask that he would, by the power of the Spirit, prepare you for even more service to him in the days ahead.

What No One Else Could Ever Do, pg. 346

Jesus Christ has done upon the cross what no priest of Israel could ever have done, and what no worldly religion can ever achieve today. For both the Hebrew Christian in danger of abandoning Christ and today's fence-sitting doubter in danger of passing by the one and true salvation, these verses sound a clanging gospel bell.

LESSON 9

HOLDING FAST TO OUR CONFESSION

Hebrews 10:19–39

THE BIG PICTURE

For several chapters the author of Hebrews has been pointing his readers' eyes back to the Old Testament—to the Levitical priesthood, the figure of Melchizedek, animal sacrifices, and regulations for old covenant worship—all with the intention of displaying the marvelous supremacy of Jesus Christ and of the full salvation he brings. Now, as this passage begins, we see the author's focus moving toward application—how must Christians respond, act, and live in light of these glorious gospel realities? First, Christians should draw near to God with "full assurance of faith" (10:22), hold fast to the truth of the gospel, and encourage one another to do the same through regular meetings and through teaching (10:19–25). Then, however, the author returns to a word of warning, sternly reminding his readers that spurning the Son of God and returning to sin is much more grievous than the rebellion of God's people in the Old Testament was, because Jesus has offered his very blood for us (10:26–31). Finally, though, we come to words of exhortation and encouragement: by faith, Christians can and will endure through hardship, suffering, and struggle (10:32–39). Followers of the risen and reigning Savior must not "shrink back" (see 10:38) but must press on toward the "great reward" that they have in Christ (10:35).

Read Hebrews 10:19–39.

GETTING STARTED

1. Why can it be so difficult to transition from having "head knowledge" about something to actually practicing it, or living it out? Can you think of some examples of this from everyday life? How has this been a struggle for you in your Christian faith?

2. How have you observed—in your neighborhood, community, or social circles—dismissive attitudes toward Jesus, Christianity, and the Bible? What eternal realities have you seen people shrug off in everyday conversation?

Therefore, pg. 358

Now, in the transition from doctrine to application he says, "Therefore, brothers." We should always take note of the Bible's "therefores," because they provide the link between cause and effect. "Therefore," the writer of Hebrews says by way of transition, what we believe must transfer into our life and actions.

OBSERVING THE TEXT

3. How is it clear, as this passage begins, that the author of Hebrews is beginning to apply the marvelous truths about Jesus Christ to the lives, hearts, and attitudes of his audience? What key words indicate that this text is moving toward application?

4. What encouraging invitations are contained in this passage? What somber warnings does it contain as well?

5. What characteristics of genuine Christianity are mentioned throughout this passage from Hebrews? How might these be helpful for your own self-evaluation?

UNDERSTANDING THE TEXT

6. What are the three main applications of Jesus's gracious salvation to which the author of Hebrews points in 10:19–25? How ought the

gospel to affect the way that we approach God? How ought it to affect the way that we cling to biblical truth?

7. How ought the gospel to shape our relationships with other Christians (10:24–25)? Why is meeting together with other Christians so important, according to these verses?

8. What kind of sin, and what accompanying attitude, does the author of Hebrews describe in 10:26? Why is it so important to distinguish this category of sin from the type of sin that does, indeed, regularly plague the lives of genuine believers in Jesus Christ?

The Outrage of Man, pgs. 375–76

That [God] should judge sinners is not the outrage; the outrage is that man, having received this gift from God, should then despise it, should trample under foot the name of Jesus as God's Son, should treat as unholy his precious blood, and should insult the Spirit of God as he bears testimony to the gospel in this world.

9. Why is the kind of sin and rebellion that 10:26 describes so particularly grievous (see also 10:27–31)? How does the author of Hebrews use the Old Testament to make a "lesser to greater" argument with regard to the effects of this kind of sin? What do we learn about the weight and value of what God has offered to his people through Jesus's work on the cross?

10. What kinds of suffering and persecution does the author of Hebrews ask his readers to recall (10:32–34)? Why does he bring these sufferings to their attention?

11. How would you summarize the exhortation that ends this passage (10:35–39)? Why might the author have chosen to use the quotation from Habakkuk that appears here, and why would his readers have found this encouraging? How are these verses directing Christians' attention toward the future hope that is theirs in Christ?

BIBLE CONNECTIONS

12. Read Habakkuk 2:2–5, which contains God's response to Habakkuk's complaint against God's use of the pagan nation of Babylon to judge

his own people. What do you notice about God's words to the prophet Habakkuk? How is God's mention that the "righteous" will live by "faith" an important reminder for believers who are in the midst of suffering and hardship?

13. In Revelation 21:1–5, the apostle John is given a vision of the new heaven and new earth—the eternal dwelling place of God and his people. How does John's vision inform our understanding of the "reward" to which the author of Hebrews points (10:35–36)?

THEOLOGY CONNECTIONS

14. Charles Spurgeon once remarked, "If I did not believe the doctrine of the final perseverance of the saints, I think I should be of all men the most miserable, because I should lack any ground for comfort."[1] How does this passage from Hebrews, and particularly verses 32–39, teach this doctrine of eternal security—or the perseverance of the saints to the end? Why does warning and exhorting believers not conflict with believing in this doctrine?

1. Charles Spurgeon, "A Happy Christian," *Sermons from Metropolitan Tabernacle Pulpit*, vol. 13, available online from The Spurgeon Center, accessed February 12, 2020, https://www.spurgeon.org/resource-library/sermons/a-happy-christian#flipbook/ .

15. The Westminster Shorter Catechism, in answer 87, defines repentance unto life as "a saving grace, whereby a sinner, out of a true sense of his sin, and apprehension of the mercy of God in Christ, doth, with grief and hatred of his sin, turn from it unto God, with full purpose of, and endeavor after, new obedience." Given this statement, why might "sinning deliberately" be evidence that this kind of repentance has never actually taken place within a person (10:26)?

APPLYING THE TEXT

16. How might this passage (and particularly 10:24–25) change and shape your interactions with other Christians in your church? In your family? Discuss ways that you might grow in "stirring up" fellow believers toward love and good works.

17. What ought to be the effect of warning passages in Scripture, such as Hebrews 10:26–31, in your life and heart? How can you respond to such a passage with proper humility, fear, and faith?

18. How ought the sufferings and persecutions of your brothers and sisters in Christ (both in the present and in the past) encourage you to persevere in your own faith? In what ways might you more regularly focus on your future reward and hope in Jesus?

PRAYER PROMPT

As you close your study of Hebrews 10:19–39, ask God to help you take to heart the applications, warnings, and encouragements that are found in these verses. Pray that the Holy Spirit would bolster your assurance as you boldly approach God's throne of grace through the finished work of Jesus. Pray for God's strength to help you to hold fast to your faith, exhort your brothers and sisters in Christ, and reject a stubborn return to the sin for which your Savior died. Finally, ask God to help you to fix your eyes on the future reward that you have in Christ; pray that he would enable you to persevere through all kinds of suffering and hardship through his gift of faith.

Perseverance in Faith, pg. 387
The same God who ordained the end of salvation for his elect also ordained the means by which we will get there, and that is perseverance in faith. Perseverance means acting in faith, and acting in faith means growing. We cannot sit still.

LESSON 10

BY FAITH

Hebrews 11:1–12:3

THE BIG PICTURE

For ten chapters, the author of Hebrews has been laying out the supreme, sufficient, and gracious salvation that Christians have in their Savior, Jesus Christ—he is the Great High Priest, the final sacrifice, and the one who secures our access to the very throne room of God! Because of these glorious truths, the author of Hebrews has so far interspersed four distinct sections of stern warnings, calling believers to persevere, to remain steadfast, and to refuse to swerve from the hope they have in Christ alone. Now, in chapter 11, we come to a glorious celebration and explanation of the core of the Christian life: *faith.* All of the promises of God in Christ are received by faith, which assures us of all that we hope for in him (11:1–3). The author of Hebrews then goes on to demonstrate, as he has many times earlier in the epistle, how believers in Jesus Christ can learn from the examples of Old Testament believers who have gone before (11:4–40). This central section of Hebrews 11 recounts how faith worked itself out in the lives of God's people throughout the ages—how it demonstrated itself in obedience, perseverance, victory, and even suffering. Believers throughout the ages have modeled for us a steadfast faith in the promises of a God whom they could not see and who promised them an eternal future that was not yet in their grasp. The conclusion, after this lengthy look back at the lives of Old Testament believers, exhorts us to allow these "witnesses" to spur us onward in faith in Jesus Christ, so that we run the race that has been set before us in him (12:1–3).

Read Hebrews 11:1–12:3.

GETTING STARTED

1. What are some ways that people in our world today mockingly describe the Christian faith and its belief in the supernatural, invisible realms, heaven and hell, and a God whom we cannot see? How do such people, ironically, place their faith in other truths or realities that they cannot see?

2. How have you sought to learn from the past (e.g., by studying history, observing the lives of friends or family members, or making use of institutional memory)?

The Life of Faith, pg. 390

The Christian life is the life of faith. Faith is the issue on which the matter of salvation depends; it is the key that turns the lock on the door to eternal life. Faith is the channel by which we receive the benefits of Christ's saving work; it is the cup into which God pours his saving grace.

OBSERVING THE TEXT

3. What do you notice about the way in which this passage begins (11:1–3) and concludes (12:1–3)? How might the beginning and ending explain to you how the author of Hebrews wants the bulk of the passage (11:4–40) to be understood and applied in the lives of his readers?

4. Notice the Old Testament people and stories that are mentioned. What surprises you about what and who is included?

5. What is encouraging about this passage from Hebrews? How is the author calling you to understand and consider believers who have gone before you?

UNDERSTANDING THE TEXT

6. What do you notice about the biblical author's definition of faith in 11:1–3? How is this different from other ways you have heard faith defined in the past? What is crucial for Christian faith, according to this definition?

7. How did Abel, Enoch, Noah, Abraham, and Sarah demonstrate their faith, according to this passage (11:4–12)? How did God respond to their faith in his promises? To what details does the author of Hebrews call our attention as he very briefly mentions these Old Testament believers?

8. What connection is there between obedient faith and future hope, according to Hebrews 11:13–16? How does the author of Hebrews describe these Old Testament believers' future-oriented focus? Toward what do they ultimately look?

9. What elements of the stories of Abraham, Jacob, Joseph, and Moses does this passage highlight (11:17–30)? How is Rahab a different "kind" of character for the author to mention (11:31)? Why might he have chosen to mention her at this point?

Faith on Display, pg. 401

Ultimately it is not these men and women who are on display, in all their variety of experience, but rather the one faith that shows its various facets in their lives. Through these historical and biblical figures, the author personifies the faith he is commending, and we thereby see all the things faith does and the benefits it conveys.

10. What is difficult about some of the people who are mentioned in Hebrews 11:32–40? What conclusions might we draw about the way in which the author of Hebrews is using the idea of "faith" throughout this passage? Why is it important to understand that the lives of faithful believers do not all look the same, with regard to suffering and earthly triumph (see 11:36–38)?

11. What is powerful about the way that Hebrews 12:1–3 concludes and applies this passage? What is the role of Jesus Christ in our lives as we seek to run the race as men and women of faith? How does his person and work guide, lead, and empower us?

BIBLE CONNECTIONS

12. Read the story of Rahab in Joshua 2:1–21. Note also the mention she receives in Matthew 1:5. Why is Rahab such a marvelous example of faith in the Old Testament? How does she actively demonstrate her faith in God? What is the wonderful result of this faith?

13. In Romans 4:1–10, the apostle Paul writes about the faith of Abraham, which came before the sign of circumcision and made him righteous in the sight of God. Read those verses carefully. How does Paul's explanation of the faith of Abraham expand on all that the author of Hebrews says about Abraham in chapter 11?

THEOLOGY CONNECTIONS

14. The Westminster Confession of Faith states that faith is "the alone instrument of justification" (11.2). How has this theological truth been made abundantly clear already in the book of Hebrews? In what ways does this passage continue to expand our understanding of faith—and of how it demonstrates itself in the lives of believers?

15. One of the hallmarks of the Reformed faith is its understanding of the continuity of the history of redemption, which runs throughout both the Old and New Testaments. The Reformed faith holds to one overarching "covenant of grace" that God makes with his people, so that believers in every age are saved by faith alone—as they either look ahead toward God's ultimate provision of Jesus or, like us, look back in faith to what Jesus accomplished on the cross. How does this passage reinforce this understanding of the continuity of God's way of salvation throughout the ages?

APPLYING THE TEXT

16. How might this passage strengthen your faith in God—particularly by defining it more precisely in biblical terms? How might God be calling you to act more decisively and clearly in a response of faith to his promises and his Word?

17. What does this passage teach Christians today about our hope in Christ—how does the future figure in to that hope? How can this chapter strengthen our faith in the midst of suffering, pain, and temptation?

18. How might you more actively and intentionally remind yourself of the "great . . . cloud of witnesses" that surround you, along with using this reminder as motivation to continue to run the race of faith (12:1)?

The Context for Believers pg. 529

If you are a believer, he says, this is the context in which you should see yourself. This is the body to which you belong, and whose approval you should court. This is the audience, as it were, before whom you live, a great arena filled with the beloved of God, the faithful of all ages, and now is the day when you are running your race to the sounds of their approval and encouragement.

PRAYER PROMPT

You have studied a very rich and well-known passage of Scripture—and have hopefully grown in your understanding and appreciation of it in the process. Today, as you close your time in Hebrews 11:1–12:3, begin by asking God to continue to deepen and strengthen your faith—your "certainty" of the unseen promises that are yours in Jesus Christ by faith (11:1). Then pray that he would impress on your mind and heart the examples of faithful believers who have gone before you as a great "cloud" to remind you of God's call to show obedience, faithfulness, and endurance even through great suffering. Finally, ask God the Father to enable you, by the power of the Holy Spirit, to look to Jesus as the author and perfecter of your faith so that you may run with endurance the race that is set before you.

LESSON 11

DISCIPLINE AND HOLINESS

Hebrews 12:4–17

THE BIG PICTURE

Even Christians who believe the right doctrinal truths about Jesus Christ and his gospel still face the danger of embracing false ideas about God if they are confronted by suffering, difficulty, or hardship. As the author of Hebrews continues his letter, he aims first to help his audience think rightly about their troubles—to understand the fatherly role that God displays in them and through them (12:7). God's people can rightly understand the trials of this life as being the "discipline" of a Father who has given his Son in order to adopt them as his own (12:5–7). This discipline is something that Christians are called to endure, accept, and see as part of God's strengthening and testing work in their lives; the discipline of the heavenly Father is not a sign of his lack of care but one of his love for his children! Ultimately, the end goal of this discipline is the "holiness" of God's people (12:10, 14). As Christians, we are called to allow God's discipline to shape us into the image of Christ rather than to allow sin and the "root of bitterness" to enter our hearts in the midst of hardship (12:15). Our passage concludes with another warning—this time from the life of Esau, who ultimately chose the pleasures of fleshly sin over the blessing of God (12:16–17). Unlike Esau, Christians must endure the discipline of God as they press on toward obedience and holiness in Christ.

Read Hebrews 12:4–17.

GETTING STARTED

1. What false claims do people often make about God when they are faced with pain, struggle, sickness, or difficulty? How have you seen people change their view of God in the midst of the hardships of life? How have others clung to faith in encouraging ways?

2. Why do Christians, who are saved by grace, still need to be warned about sin, unbelief, and rebellion? How has the author of Hebrews modeled effective warning thus far in this letter?

Divine Discipline, pg. 541

These verses . . . speak of divine discipline: the biblical teaching that God chastises and trains his children by means of the difficulties and hardships of life. This is a topic we hardly care about when God does not seem to be doing it; but when his hand of chastisement falls, Christians greatly need the encouragement and instruction found here.

OBSERVING THE TEXT

3. Based on your initial reading of this passage, what false views might the author of Hebrews be writing to correct? What can you learn about these erroneous perspectives based on the corrections that the author offers?

4. Notice the extended comparison this passage makes between God and good earthly fathers (12:5–10). Why is this such a helpful analogy for us? How is it a difficult analogy for some Christians?

5. What are some of God's ultimate purposes for his people that are revealed throughout this passage?

UNDERSTANDING THE TEXT

6. Why might the author of Hebrews have chosen to quote from the particular proverb that he quotes in 12:5–6? What does it tell us about how we should understand the discipline we receive from God? How is this the opposite of what people sometimes assume about God's discipline?

7. What are the intended effects of God's discipline of us, according to Hebrews 12:10–11? How might an understanding of this "fruit" that discipline produces give us increased endurance and encouragement even in the midst of hardship?

8. How do verses 12–13 conclude the section of this passage about God's discipline of his children? How do they also connect to the next section (12:14–17)? How might you summarize the call, or exhortation, that the author of Hebrews makes in these verses?

9. What is surprising about the call for us to have "peace" with everyone that comes in Hebrews 12:14? What does this tell us about the role and demeanor of Christians in this world as well as about the connection between peaceful living and "holiness" (12:14)?

God's Holy Intentions, pg. 548

What a difference it makes to realize that God, who is good, has only good for us in his manner of discipline. However difficult it is for us to perceive, he is making "all things work together for good" in our lives (Rom. 8:28). Since God is holy, all his intentions for us are also holy. They are pure, they are for our benefit, and they bring credit to him.

10. What are the three distinct dangers that the author of Hebrews warns against in 12:15–16? Why might he have chosen to mention these specific sins to his readers?

11. How does the Old Testament example of Esau prove to be a poignant accompaniment to the third danger that the author of Hebrews warns his readers about (12:16–17)? What is it about Esau, specifically, that is mentioned? Why was his remorse ineffective—and too late?

BIBLE CONNECTIONS

12. Read a bit more about Esau, in both Genesis 25:29–34 and Genesis 36:1–5. How would you describe this man, simply from reading these two brief passages? What hints do you find that he may have been controlled by his own appetites rather than by the clear Word of God?

13. Paul writes about the sufferings and hardships of this life as being preparatory as well—read 2 Corinthians 4:16–18. How does Paul describe the sufferings of life in a fallen world? In what ways does he connect

such suffering and hardship to the eternal glory that lies ahead for us in Christ?

THEOLOGY CONNECTIONS

14. The Puritan theologian John Owen, in his *Exposition of the Epistle to the Hebrews,* wrote, "When, by the wisdom of God, we can discern that what we suffer on the one hand is for the glory of God and the gospel, and on the other is necessary unto our own sanctification, we shall be prevailed with unto patience and perseverance."[1] How can the truths we have studied about God's good purposes behind his discipline increase our patience and perseverance?

15. The answer to question 35 of the Westminster Shorter Catechism offers this definition of sanctification: "Sanctification is the work of God's free grace, whereby we are renewed in the whole man after the image of God, and are enabled more and more to die unto sin, and live unto righteousness." What is so encouraging about this definition of sanctification, and particularly of what empowers it, in light of the strong call toward holiness that you have just studied in Hebrews 12:14–17?

1. John Owen, *An Exposition of the Epistle to the Hebrews,* ed. W. H. Goold (New York, 1855), 7:252–53.

APPLYING THE TEXT

16. How does this passage call for you to adjust your thinking about painful challenges in your life? In what ways are you tempted to think that God is displeased with you when pain comes—instead of remembering that, if you are in Christ, perhaps the very opposite is true?

17. In what way could this passage better, and more biblically, shape your prayer life during seasons of trials? How could you pray for holiness and righteousness more earnestly in the midst of periods of discipline?

18. How ought this passage to warn you against the dangers of failing to obtain the grace of God, allowing the root of bitterness to grow, and falling prey to sexual sin? In what ways can your church, and the Christians around you, support you as you seek to stand against these temptations?

Our Reasons for Holiness, pg. 563
The life in store for us is a holy life. Therefore, let us make every effort to be holy, for it is with holiness that someday we will see our precious Lord, and it is with holiness that others can see him now in us.

PRAYER PROMPT

This passage has invited Christians to consider God as their good heavenly Father—one who has designed even trials and pain to be his chosen discipline for the children he loves. Today, pray that God would enable you to see his discipline as just that, so that you may endure through it and be built up in holiness and righteousness. Pray for his strength and protection against sin, too, and invite his power to enable you to strive toward holiness with all your effort, love, and might.

LESSON 12

UNSHAKEABLE MOUNTAIN

Hebrews 12:18–29

THE BIG PICTURE

As we have seen so often already in our study of Hebrews, the book's author sets out to establish the supremacy, sufficiency, and all-surpassing glory of the salvation that believers receive through Jesus Christ, God's Son, when they believe his gospel. As this passage begins, the author again makes this point by comparing two biblically significant mountains: Mount Sinai and Mount Zion (12:18–24). Sinai represents the law, which was given by Moses and accompanied by great glory. Zion, though, represents the gospel, which was brought forth by Jesus Christ himself, who mediates a "new covenant" with God's people through his blood (12:24). It is to this glorious and heavenly "mountain" that believers in Jesus Christ come by faith. This glorious invitation leads the author of Hebrews to make yet another word of warning: judgment came against God's people in the Old Testament when they rebelled against his Word—so how much more will his judgment fall on people who reject his own Son (12:25–29)? The right response of faithful Christians is to receive, by faith, this great kingdom of God that cannot be shaken—and to worship the all-holy God with reverence and awe (12:28). Indeed, this is the only appropriate response to the God and Father of our Lord and Savior Jesus Christ!

Read Hebrews 12:18–29.

GETTING STARTED

1. Have you ever struggled with becoming "bored" with the Christian faith, with God's Word, or even with God himself? If so, what helped you to snap out of it? What truths reminded you of the wonder of your salvation, the goodness of God, and the sweetness of his Word?

2. Why might some people today tend to have a more casual familiarity with God rather than a sense of reverence and awe? How might you, and those in your community, need to be reminded of the holiness, glory, and awe-inspiring power of the creator God?

Contrasts, pg. 565

It is not to Mount Sinai in the desert that Christians are told that they have come. Mount Sinai is brought into the picture, but only to present a contrast by which the mount of our salvation may be seen more clearly. It is a contrast between Sinai and Zion, between Moses and Christ, between the law and the gospel.

OBSERVING THE TEXT

3. How is faith in Jesus Christ and his gospel contrasted in this passage with all that came before it? What is it, specifically, about the glory of the gospel that so surpasses the glory of the Old Testament law that was given through Moses?

4. Notice the focus that the author places on the theme of mountains—particularly in 12:20–22. Why are these mountains important? What do they symbolize?

5. What seem to be the main exhortations in this passage? What is the concluding warning—and how does it follow from the truths of the passage?

UNDERSTANDING THE TEXT

6. How does the author of Hebrews describe the glory and holiness that surrounded the giving of the law on Mount Sinai (12:18–21)? What

should the frightening holiness of that moment teach us about God? About human sinfulness?

7. What is different about Mount Zion, which Christians approach through faith in Jesus (12:22–23)? In what ways does its glory so obviously surpass the glory of Mount Sinai? How does this teach us about the gospel and about its relationship to the Old Testament law?

8. What is the role of Jesus Christ in this second "mountain," and why is his role such a significant part of its greater glory (12:24)? Why might the author make reference to Abel?

Your Current Reality, pgs. 572–73

This is not merely a picture of your future reality—this is now your reality if you are a Christian. You have come to this mountain, where the threatening flames burn no more. You have come to this city, in which the worship of angels surrounds the people of God. You have come to this church, vindicated by God, proclaimed righteous and made perfect in Christ.

9. What makes it obvious that 12:25–29 is the "application" of 12:18–24 (see vv. 25, 28)? How do the glorious truths of this gospel "mountain" naturally lead into a grave and weighty warning?

10. What argument is being made, in 12:25–26, with regard to God's judgment in the Old Testament as well as his judgment on those who reject the gospel today? How is this an effective "lesser to greater" argument?

11. How ought we to approach God, according to 12:28–29? What must we understand about his character and holiness? What must we remember about our inheritance, which we receive through faith in Jesus Christ?

BIBLE CONNECTIONS

12. Read Exodus 19:7–20. How is the frightening glory of God described to us in this passage, as he descends on Mount Sinai? Why is it important for us to understand this revelation of God's character and blinding holiness?

13. Paul writes of the "fading" glory of the law, which was revealed even in Moses's shining face, in 2 Corinthians 3:7–11. How does that passage serve as a complement to the one we are studying in this lesson? What else does it teach about the glory of the law—and the greater glory of Christ's gospel?

THEOLOGY CONNECTIONS

14. Question 18 of the Heidelberg Catechism asks who the "Mediator" for God's people is, and this answer is given: "Our Lord Jesus Christ, who was made unto us wisdom from God, and righteousness and sanctification, and redemption." How does this answer explain how Jesus is the "mediator of a new covenant," as Hebrews 12:24 asserts?

15. Within traditional Reformed thought, the "first use" of the law is understood to be as a kind of mirror—one that shows us both the holiness and righteousness of God and the sinfulness and fallenness of humanity. How might this "first use" of the law help to explain the reactions of the law's recipients in Hebrews 12:19–20?

APPLYING THE TEXT

16. How ought this text to shake you out of spiritual lethargy or boredom? What do you need to remember about your own salvation—especially based on 12:18–24?

17. What reaction do you have to this passage's "lesser to greater" argument regarding God's judgment on those who reject his kingdom (12:25–26)? How might you apply this warning to your life for your own spiritual benefit?

18. How should this passage shape the way you daily approach God in prayer, worship, and petition (12:28–29)? Why might you need to grow in your sense of "awe and reverence" before God?

Fear and Thanksgiving, pg. 583

As creatures before the Creator, we must tremble with fear, we must reckon on his holiness with a godly awe that produces reverence in all our dealings with him. But to awe we must add thanksgiving. We are sinners redeemed by the hand of mercy, enemies who are reconciled by love, rebels who are made children and heirs of God's eternal kingdom.

PRAYER PROMPT

This is a passage that ought to shake us out of holding any deficient views of the salvation we have in Jesus Christ! The frightening glory that surrounded Mount Sinai as God gave his law to his people through Moses is far surpassed by the glory of Mount Zion, onto which we have been invited by the Son of God himself. Today, pray that God would give you a greater appreciation and richer understanding of the kingdom that you enter by the blood of his Son. Ask him for awe and reverence as you consider the access that you now have to the holy God of the universe, in whose presence you can forever dwell.

LESSON 13

LIVES OF PRAISE TO JESUS

Hebrews 13:1–25

THE BIG PICTURE

As the author of Hebrews concludes his letter, he draws upon many themes that have become quite familiar to us: the unchanging glory of Jesus, his final sacrifice for sins, and the importance of holiness in the Christian life. He is also at his most practical in this chapter, giving concrete and explicit commands to Christians as they consider their everyday lives as followers of Jesus. We can understand this chapter as a call to live lives of praise to Jesus—in the community of believers (13:1–8), in the eyes of a watching and often hostile world (13:9–14), and finally in the sight of God himself, who calls us to serve others and respect the leaders he has placed over us (13:15–19). Finally, the book of Hebrews concludes with a moving word of benedictory blessing as it asks the same God who raised Jesus from the dead to equip his people to please him in every way (13:20–21). The clear picture that emerges from Hebrews 13 is one of lives that are shaped in every way by the gospel of Jesus Christ. Christians who have put their faith in him will be marked by the way in which they love and serve those around them, endure humbly the reproach of the world, rejoice in praising their God, respect their God-given leaders, and share boldly the gospel hope that is theirs in Jesus.

Read Hebrews 13:1–25.

GETTING STARTED

1. Have you, or others you know, struggled with the reality of "unloving" Christians in certain contexts? Why is it such a sad testimony to the Christian faith when brothers and sisters in Christ hurt, insult, and lash out against one another?

2. Why is it so difficult to stand out, or to be counted as "weird" or "different," for the sake of Jesus Christ? How have you felt the pressure to conform to the pattern of the culture around you—in your neighborhood, workplace, or social circles?

You Serve Christ Himself, pg. 594

If you are a Christian, these commands are not given as just some ideal or program, some bygone philosophy that served a prior generation. Rather, by this kind of life, you are now serving and following Jesus Christ himself, who was and is and is to come, who lives and reigns now in the heavens and by his Spirit on the earth.

OBSERVING THE TEXT

3. How do this chapter's rapid-fire commands regarding the Christian life flow logically out of the final verses of Hebrews 12? Why is it not "random" for the author of Hebrews to move toward practical instructions and applications for the church at this point in the letter?

4. In what ways is Jesus Christ held up as our example throughout this passage? How does the person of Jesus impact our behavior toward others? How does his example shape our endurance in the midst of a hostile world?

5. What observations do you make about the way that the author of Hebrews chooses to conclude this letter? On what does he focus in his benediction? What people does he mention in the final verses—and why?

UNDERSTANDING THE TEXT

6. What do you notice about the particular commands that are given to Christians in Hebrews 13:1–7? What do they have in common? What relationships do they address? How does verse 8 relate to these commands as well as pointing forward to verses 9–14?

7. What hints do you get about the kinds of "diverse and strange teachings" that the author of Hebrews warns against in 13:9? How is the sacrifice of Jesus Christ then contrasted with religious rituals and the accompanying obsession with foods (13:9–12)?

8. How does the author of Hebrews use the example of Jesus to encourage believers who are marginalized, mocked, or alienated (13:12–13)? What is the significance of Jesus's suffering "outside the camp," and how does that apply to the lives that Christians live in a fallen world today?

A General Rule, pg. 604

We cannot be sure what the exact problem was among the Hebrews, yet we see in the answer a principle we may use as a general rule. Unless a system of religion relies utterly on the work of Christ in his substitutionary work of atonement, it is alien, it is foreign, to the true religion of Scripture, which is by grace alone, through faith alone, in Christ alone, and especially in his redeeming blood.

9. What is so helpful about the command in Hebrews 13:15? Why might this verse be a good summary for the entire Christian life?

10. Why might a call to obedience and submission to spiritual leaders come at this point (13:17)? How does this call relate to the previous call for us to live sacrificially in praise to Jesus? In what ways does the author of Hebrews invite his audience to pray for him and the other church leaders specifically (13:18–19)?

11. How does this epistle's benediction make reference to some familiar themes from earlier on (13:20–21)? What is meant to be encouraging about this concluding blessing? How is the epistle's audience called to respond to and receive this letter (12:22)?

BIBLE CONNECTIONS

12. Read Galatians 6:1–10, which contains practical instructions for how Christians should live with and serve each other in the body of Christ. What similarities does this passage have with the commands in the

opening verses of Hebrews 13? What different instructions does it include?

13. Joshua 1:5 is quoted directly in Hebrews 13:5. Go back to Joshua 1, and note the surrounding context of that verse. Why might the author of Hebrews have chosen that particular verse to quote in the midst of his instructions to the church?

THEOLOGY CONNECTIONS

14. The oft-quoted first question of the Westminster Shorter Catechism ("What is the chief end of man?") is accompanied by this answer: "Man's chief end is to glorify God and to enjoy him forever." How is the essence of this truth captured in the command that is given in Hebrews 13:15?

15. In many churches within the Reformed tradition, new members make a covenant to respect, honor, and obey the elders of that church. How does our passage today point to this as being a worthy call and command (13:17)? Why is respect for leaders important evidence of submission to Jesus and devotion to God?

APPLYING THE TEXT

16. As you look back through the practical exhortations that appear in Hebrews 13:1–7, which ones convict you the most right now? How should these commands call you toward deeper love, generosity, hospitality, or gentleness?

17. What keeps you from embracing marginalization and mockery for the sake of Jesus Christ and his gospel? How have you been guilty of keeping silent about Jesus because of fear or shame? In what ways does the suffering and shame of Jesus need to shape your bold witness for him more significantly?

The Greatest of Blasphemies, pgs. 629–30

In light of the cross of Christ, the accusation that God is far off and aloof from the reality of this world is in fact the greatest of all blasphemies. For the cross displays God's involvement in the world in a way that is not only far greater than we could demand, but is far more gracious than we could imagine. . . . He also entered into our world in the person of his Son, spilling his own blood and taking death onto himself that he might seek and save those who were lost.

18. How might you offer a "sacrifice of praise" to God more fully this week (13:15)? What might that look like in your family, your relationships, your church, or your community?

PRAYER PROMPT

This final chapter of the book of Hebrews reminds us that, when we truly embrace the gospel of Jesus Christ and place our faith in him, our entire lives are meant to be lived as sacrifices of praise to our Savior. Today, pray that God would continually transform your relationships with those around you—and particularly with those in your church community. Ask him to enable you to live boldly for Jesus before the eyes of a watching world, as you remember the shame and suffering and mockery that your Savior endured for you. Finally, pray that God would continue to equip you to live all of life as a joyful sacrifice to him, who sent forth his own Son as a sacrifice for you!

Jon Nielson is senior pastor of Spring Valley Presbyterian Church in Roselle, Illinois, and the author of *Bible Study: A Student's Guide,* among other books. He has served in pastoral positions at Holy Trinity Church, Chicago, and College Church, Wheaton, Illinois, and as director of training for the Charles Simeon Trust.

Richard D. Phillips (MDiv, Westminster Theological Seminary; DD, Greenville Presbyterian Theological Seminary) is the senior minister of Second Presbyterian Church of Greenville, South Carolina. He is a council member of the Alliance of Confessing Evangelicals and of The Gospel Coalition and chairman of the Philadelphia Conference on Reformed Theology.